ALL THE WORDS A STAGE

A Chameleon Press Book

ALL THE WORDS A STAGE
ISBN 978-988-16629-4-1

Published by Chameleon Press, Hong Kong
www.chameleonpress.com

First printing 2018

ALL THE WORDS A STAGE

POETRY BY NASHUA GALLAGHER

chameleon press
hong kong

Contents

Section One
"Stage": a point, period, or step in a process or development

Section Two

"Stage": a raised floor or platform, typically in a theatre, on which actors, entertainers, or speakers perform

For Angus, Kian & Adara

"There's no place like home"
— The Wizard of Oz

Preface

Apparently a good pun does not need to be explained. But this title is no joke.

I like puns, and I like words, and many of them made their way to a stage as they developed through different phases in my life. Incidentally, I like Shakespeare too.

This is a story from ages sixteen to twenty-something, set in a tall city on an autumn Wednesday evening in late 2005. It began when a girl, who sometimes studied and sometimes worked, made her way to a tiny unassuming cafe and bar tucked away in one of the side streets of Hong Kong's Soho district and gave voice to some of the words in this book. I hadn't intended for them to move beyond paper, or from between the (then) electric blue walls of Joyce Is Not Here, Artists Bar and Café. Nor could I have anticipated how this weekly gathering amongst friends would grow into a beloved literary collective now known as Peel Street Poetry.

This collection is comprised in two parts—stage—that refers to a step in a process and—stage—which refers to the platform in which to exhibit or share. One is naturally introspective, the other outward-looking. This so happens to be how the poems in this collection naturally progressed.

From the saccharine tenderness of a great love in its infancy, the bitter dulling of friendships lost, the unexpected swelling of a belly (twice), the mundane perils of adult life, minor political rants, a love affair with an unforgiving city, and a good smattering of everything that lies between.

Semi-autobiographical, semi-chronological, these words were the candid camera at the ready, and the poems the many rolls of film that caught them. Thanks for flicking through.

Nashua Gallagher
March 2018
Hong Kong

stage

steɪdʒ/

noun

1.

a point, period, or step in a process or development.

synonyms: phase, period, juncture, step, point, time, moment, instant, division, level

"a stage in the development"

STAGE I

The girl stumbled upon her tribe

From stardust they came.
The sparkiest,
Onomatopoeic bang -
Hanging clefs waiting for notes to stop by.

Lens flares and love letters,
Coffee stains and guitar strings,
Passport stamps, biscuit tins.

They shark the salt waters of adult life,
Steer with grit,
Polished wit,
Opened books -
And doors.

Nomad Child

Born to a town swaddled in verdancy,
Dusty roads, colonial trims, palms waved gently in cool mountain wind,
I recall best of all its many hands -
Often feminine, deft, conjuring -
A whiff of spice, plaiting oiled hair, a burn from an iron like a rosebud on skin,
A lake, often green, deep and still.

Cooling tea in a saucer,
Clouds of red earth under running slippers,
Mango flesh sucked through a small hole in its hide,
Blood promises with trees,
Kitchen cacophonies,
This was childhood at the start of my remembering.

I was taken next to a city of cut stone and bedrock,
Where mountains pulse, under gleaming towers,
Neon puddles, and sizzling oil in open woks at the market,
Growing pains from walking through expanses of shopping arcades,
A ferry-crossing harbour bejewelled with light.

The tallest city in the world, that much taller to a child.
But it never made me feel small.

There was kindness, open palmed, as familiar as an army of aunts,
The egg waffle seller, with packets so hot each bite produced dragon breath,
All clucks and smiles, waving away my $5 coin.
The bookshop assistants who left me to it, cross-legged in a pile,
Mango, juiced, in a plastic takeaway cup, to accompany small, tired feet.

Home was a place I found on either side of the handover,
I never found a need for roots, for fear of them paved over.

July 1st 1997 was the day that Hong Kong's sovereignty changed hands from British to Chinese rule. This day is commonly referred to as the handover.

Mother Tongue

Language recall
is like parts of a peppercorn going through a sieve
caught in the back of your throat,
Sounds falter, and become the pause before the mother of all sneezes -
I emphasize with billowing gestures
build a crescendo in the lull,
Create with hands, the meaning
in the space
where my sentence trailed
and words really ought to be.

Keeping Up Appearances

The thing is,
I didn't have the luxury of the damn cup,
Half, full, or empty.

Life was temporary, in hotel rooms and spare spaces,
Caught in a newton's cradle of a man chasing dreams by dressing the part,
And a woman forced to darn the frays.

Yet -
His conviction,
Her perseverance,
Made up the bulk of my inheritance.

For awhile we thrived in the newness,
Egg fried rice with spring onion, steamed fish,
Leafy choi, and tiny dried shrimp,

Eventually, for variety,
We started ordering in curry.

My makeshift school of what-ifs and hard knocks,
Lead me to the wrong crowd and the right books,
Became a library refugee,

Bellhops would stare quizzically,
Wonder if we were still good for a tip,
But that's what worked best with hotel living -
We were not the only ones keeping up appearances.

I'm with Stupid

Academia gave me motion sickness,
Playing hopscotch with school years,
A one trick pony escaping the circus.

Chip on my shoulder,
- sized just right,
To carry the world.

Tag - you're it.
Just that half step too slow,
If knowledge were a tree, others plugged into higher branches,
I strung along like creepers on its base.

Those tendrils, though sparse and weedy grew.
Around the trunk, scaled boughs and limbs,
Affixed me to the whole, goddamn, forest.

I don't blame you for turning to the comfort of a cliché,
When you call me street smart,
At times I felt imposter turned spy,
More chip than shoulder,
More mule than pony,

Yes, I faked it all,
But learned it well.

Because I had an education -
Just one that couldn't be bought.

Bus Stop

An hour or so ago,
Fingers massaged ivory,
I sat, poking stuffing back into the cracks of the leather sofa,
The wind shushing the ripples in my coffee.

Notes, rang - soft and sober,
Time stopped to catch his breath -
Your touch from a day or so ago fills the gap.

The whole sky seemed to sigh, and raindrops fell.

Now I stand here, feet drenched by passing cars,
Humidity elasticating my hair,
Water dribbling from the corrugated rafters,
A bus stop
None the special -
Except for the thoughts I have of you.

Blue – For Joyce is Not Here

I want to talk to you about the warmest blue I know.
The little room where coffee rings grew cold,
Ballpoint blue flecks on fingers stained long,
And they said I could never grow old.

At 16 I wrote;
"Let's sit within the tonality of a blue-tinged harmony,
A young sky thickened by its five o' clock shadow,
The bronze of conversation coats our cheeks,
A smile borrowed from this moment will later ignite others
And together we will find the first digit of infinity."

This - was the sweetest blue,
Fold in its hue and deepen with the day,
Cherry red cheeks as the night came thick and fast,
From afternoon to evening, in vino veritas,

The faces I can eke out from any crowd,
Diamonds in the rough, rough grinding day by day -
But on a Wednesday night;
Words flowed, slow, set carefully,
Verse held by a ring of faces,
Polished to a shine,

This was just the beginning, though we didn't know it at the time.

At 17 I wrote;
"Coffee assumes that void when the season's flavour is distilled,
As this flurried ink baptizes paper with my still-born thoughts.
I am engulfed in the navy of a sky that remains starless
Even in the absence of city light."

Joyce is not here Artist's Bar & Café was the original home of Peel Street Poetry, a literary arts collective,

I got blue like the blues here, too.
We listened to Louis, and bolero
Told stories of pain and plucked them like fishbones from our rib-cages.
From loneliness's throb
To snorting laughter like the drug it became.

They stripped the blue from those walls.
I scratched out the child and in a trick of time we both grew.
They broke the bricks in and I straightened my back,
Heard every iteration of;
'What do you want to be when you grow up?'
Until I got here, and they stopped asking.

I'll remember the blue.

More than the watercolour smear of limbs on the wall,
The perfume in the toilet,
Cracks in the leather,
Legs on my table,
The grind of the coffee,
The books on the makeshift shelves,
The voices I know to read in their words
The slope that tilted as my heels grew,
The deep fried squid from next door,
The puffs of conversation outside,
The mulled, red wine.
Their faces, as I walked down the aisle.

I'll remember the blue,
And it will be hot inside my head,
We'll weave our yarns, till they're thick,
Like a blanket to sit with a friend,
And drink deep from a glass that always refills,
As though Joyce was here.

Fold-Out bed

A mechanical frame sets my spine every night,
As dreams arrive,
I wait in line,
For thoughts to dissolve with urban light.

I remember,
A bed as soft and stern as the wrinkled hands
that laid the sheets,
Pointing to a picture, creased
Seventeen-year-old school smile,
My mother's face has changed,
Outside that blue plastic frame,
And her aunt's hands bound inside the sheets
Of a farewell white.

Gone, two years now
My foreign tongue fell awry to her ears,
The sound of white echoes softly in its dearth.

I can't collate the thoughts I know little about,
The diverge of who she thought I was when she died,
And where I placed her when she was alive,

My iron wrought cot groans - It's late,
Perspiration leaks, sweat cold in the heat.
She was the first of four sisters, you know
I am one of three,
I suppose the difference between life and death,
Is all what separates memory from legacy.

Then there's us and time,
Whether we know it or not - in line,
to get to the other side.

Did she know that I never meant to leave her behind?

Untitled For When You Were Away

A pale dusk lacquers the atmosphere,
As the sun wades into the backwaters of time,

Darkness begins his rounds,
Solitude - no longer an indulgence
When it's no longer a choice.

Passing by Mong Kok

Night feels thick against my skin,
Inside a thuggish bus ride,
Ramshackle starts and stops,
Lending glimpses of the evening playbill.

China dolls, sashaying porcelain hips,
Pretty-girl gaze ovate,
Preying, praying, surveying,
Waste-not, want-nots.

Kids, flew the nest to the nearest branch,
Cigarette perched, hair-slicked, trilling laughter,
Blared lights from inside the nightclub,
Stanching shadows, swallow them in.

This granddad, he coughs next to me -
Thoughts wearing valleys through his scalp,
He sits slumped, vibrations animate jowl and gut,
Neon dances on his sleeping form,

My thoughts, now too, a plaything of the city.
Watching rapt, eyes shot wide,
The tale of our lives just passing by,
Our lives just passing by...

Your Smile Spreads

Your smile spreads like a gas leak,
And I with no match in hand,
To ignite a wrath smothered deep by;
Returned salutations,
Incriminating obligations,
Because, even your ash,
Collected in deposits,
On memory's floor,
Will snag at my thoughts
once you are no more.

Lunch Box

Do you know about cellophane love?
How tuna pockets have been basil'd, paprika'd, baked.
She is all limbs,
Flayed on our fold out,
Her mother on a distant plane,
Away.

The cellophane I wrap like a present,
To suffocation. Chocolate buttons, grapes,
To be washed down with a snug packed Ribena.
This lunch is strange, even to me.

I was given bread.
Bread with fried egg,
Stale by noon, smothered with butter, oily film to the tongue -
Biting, pepper-corned clump-like bread.

I know of spaces I tried to fill as a child
And so my lunchbox rarely returned half-full.

It wasn't lunch anyway,
It was compensation,
A thin sandwich, not to fill, but sate you,
The only lunch worth having is uncovered, fresh.

It is warmed at the hearth at home.

I would have a plate,
4.30 PM
Rice. Meat. Vegetables.
Not like you think.

Coconut milk, a base not a flavour,
Cumin, Turmeric, a leaf maybe.

She does not chuck it all in.
The powders serve a purpose.

They spill like sand,
We are coastal, we have simple needs.

I stand by the kitchen sink and think of my mother's hands,
And the many bellies it filled.
My sister stirs in the yellow beam that has fallen on her face.
I turn off the light,
Forcing us closer to the neon blimp of our mother's flight.

Midnight Tai Tais, Lan Kwai Fong

Cigarette smoke rises to heavens,
As if it serves much use up there.
Stilettos snap, cleavage dips, tummies tucked
and dresses hitched,

Thin beams hack, music thumps,
Night sways, sighs, unwinds,
Whisked on magic carpet rides, to
where dreams won't expire,
Pumpkins remain coaches
for as long as one desires.

Ring tans swathed,
Glasses clink,
For the magic to work you must not blink.
Who brought the spoil-sport, stifling a yawn?

Head bopping, playing along,
Dipping my toes into the shallows of a song,
Thinking of a man, half a day behind -
Arms outstretched, in case I fall.

Old Man (For Keith)

The phosphorous cackles,
and so he goes, into his sublime,
Leaving a backflow of dizzying wiles,
My old man, of a different kind,
As our grins waver with the retreating tide.

When We First Got Together

When we first got together,
I would urge days to roll into months,
So I could play connect the dots with memory,
And say, 'Look at the constellation he has given me!'

Could I have known then,
That I will no longer count the days we've been together,
But look to the night sky, watching the slow burn of young stars,

Brighter than manmade light,
And wish for that sort of after-life.

Orange

Hitched a ride on morning's coat tails.
Wily footfalls padded at the door,
Orange pinpricks light the stirrings below,
Apricot skies, slink traitorously through my window.

First light, lethargically unwinds,
Diffused orange still in half-slumber,
A lukewarm tinge in the distance,
Tiptoes across horizon's spread.

Lampposts and road signals flicker,
Orange peels away into the blue,
Yolk spills into a dearth,
A dawn sky succumbs to day.

I am not dressed for the occasion.
Induced by tangerine-sweet sleep,
Lashes shrivel in the coldness of day breaking,

And all I had to dream, carried on in black and white.

Nights

Nights are for the ones like me,
When quiet and cool fall on our streets,

Where alleyways lie still in wait,
Dreamers light pyres, then a wake,

Clutter cut by shuttered shops,
Construction stills, and voices drop.

A poet, restless, picks up her pen,
Inks directions for dawn's wrens.

STAGE I

The girl finds her nouns

When your name gains a pronoun,
Then your body draws on stripes,
You court people, places and do things
To put the world to rights.

Writer's Block

Black ink
White paper
Contours sit
Pleasantly splattered
Between neat bold lines

From the splatters
A zebra appears
timid, trepid, obsolete

And in these words
All I can see
Caged between
Neat bold lines

A Zebra obsolete.

Read Handed

My mother glanced over as I read,
Spine oystered, book cradled,
Eyes-shining - "Islam!" she exclaimed.

"No, Mum, it says *slam*"
At the bookstore I thumbed through it
and it felt like... foreshadowing,
It has no I, except for me.

Ideas on this sheet,
Tattooed clean,
Hidden pangs from the first cut of ink,
Oh Ma, it has slipped under my skin,
Bold, black and bare-faced, these words,
Like your little girl are *not* just to be seen, but heard.

Blackout

The novelty of a lit candle,
Licks of light, puppy-dog like, caricatured against the wall.
Its body grows shorter, and my shadow longer.

In a lone room, in a lone city,
As the solitary flames flick with my writing arm,
Body cradled to the left, pen tapping in tandem.

a slow
suspended,
slide,

of travelling wax, abruptly dry,

Much like your voice,
A flicker of hope, snuffing the most cancerous of fears.
Leaving me stumped.

Soon to be Named

There's a sewed-in harbour at my bedside;
Words are laced in the deadening night,
Far and suspended, a pendulum
between mouth and heart,
These feelings a palpable choking hazard.

And whether or not, my feet tread
a thousand-thousand pavement cracks, and face
A thousand-thousand words; that can like shrapnel shear
until my resolve is pulp on a sieve, strained
a thousand-thousand times and throbbing of
their noxious sting,

And whether or not these thoughts will itch,
And blare, and leech,
And gnaw, and weigh, and
Break my back,
Whether or not I stepped on a crack;

And whether or not, my confidence shrivels,
My belly will swell.

And this is why my feet may shuffle, but won't falter,
And my back though burdened is straight,
And the shrapnel has no edge to my resolve,
And words can be spun and spat in their haggard form,
And that will be all.

Because my heart beats, as
does yours.

Child.

The Specialist

I kept the letter from the doctor,
It got heavier every year,
A paper's weight that held my fate,
Only to become a plot twist.

I tucked it in our memory box,
With love letters, Christmas cards, ultrasounds,
First white with surrender,
Yellowed like a bruise,
Then pangs of guilt, black and blue.

He *handled it well*, I thought,
As my life walked to the corner store for a pack of cigarettes, and never came back.
I was sorry for the trouble,
Our eyes not meeting,
Silence enveloped his recommendation; go see a specialist.

My hands balled foetal, holding an invisible pen,
Watching his words spin in looped, medical script.
What it said,
I couldn't hide,
From the front,
Or the side,

I *wished* for a second opinion.
Perhaps behind rows of white prescription pills,
The nurse's nervous clipboard taps,
Was a single line doubled in error.

When tectonic worries surfaced,
He became interested in a crack in the linoleum,
Tremors broke, he cleared his throat,
Thrust the letter forward - *'the specialist would "take care of it" for me.'*

I really think that's what did it.
The seismic pause that followed,
A blink - during the eye of the storm,

I smoothed the lump from my throat,
Folded the envelope,
Tucked it in my coat,
BECAME the specialist.
Took care of it.

Kian

Would my edges harden, as you arrive to soften the blows of later life?
Will silences collect into stone, into pebbled conversation at dinner-time?

Do you know yet, that you are mine?
Little one, in all your waded glory;

With little more than a heartbeat - to recommend you to life.

Tremors of nostalgia come to mind,
When I was the gibbous moon before you arrived.

And then you bore into me with a sapphire stare
Those lips curved slight, daddy's eyes -

And when you arrived, you were recognised.

Pride spilled softly from weary, sleepy eyes,
But it was with love, that you startled us blind.

Spatial Awareness

Sleep curdles, into the mind's wake,
It is just I, a stagnant screen and the widening
distance between
Eye
        and
                the
                        mind.
A masochistic determination,
Swathed into the deepening night.

Your sleep looks like a free-fall.
Past wailing stars, a light humidity in the
Air, you breathe as though nothing is there.
Your eyes shriveled and small,
Soaked rich in the colour of sleep,

I am quite dismissed by your peace.

We awake to the wail of the morning,
Cold, yellow light.
I turn to the face of eyes green - ripe,

And close the distance, from
a drained, vacant night.

Monday

A cold cup of tea epitomizes a missed opportunity,
And I have my mugs stacked.

There are noises that may have been voices,
Swelling and ebbing beyond the backlight of my screen,

There is cadence in routine.

Restraint in a papercut,
Silence on the surface of sleep.

Tuesday.

Bathtime

The comforting scald,
A gentle broil,
My novel fallen to the wayside.

Hair billowing, then lank -
F l o a t i n g but tethered to their squeals.

A floor up, the passageway of pipes ringing with laughter,
Giggles trickle like beads of water,

"liar liar cats on fire."
I can make no correction, comment or suggestion.
Ears humming,
To feel and not be seen,
To know and not be known,

Motherhood reduced to a spectator sport,
A supporting character approaching the end of her chapter.
More or less how it's supposed to be.

Workhorse on Holiday

Hong Kong 2011
High heels clip clop on marble.
Cobblestone corns, irksome, small.
Body folds with the day,
Trudging, exhausted, homeward.

The mind a whooshing lift, pressure cooker hiss -
And escape.

London 2011
My eye falls to the scaffolds of architecture,
More wide than tall, intricate,
Peripherals survey places lived in before and after my time.

I've seen you before Mr. Ben and Parliament, Thames and Tate,
On screens and books, with text and ink, dropped in conversation,
We're like Internet friends meeting for the first time,

You're a strange sandstone sepia in the sun.
The streets bubble and squeak, skin cacophony,
Busking hustling personality, and I fold into you
Like a friend turned lover,

I saw Monet, subtle, Water Lily blur
- not stating the obvious like the crisp
card brochure, I saw Ai Wei Wei, politically
unshackled, but the best came earliest

When I saw Wordsworth, but not on a page.

Narnia (Post London 2011 *Riots, From Hong Kong)*
The forgotten Susan Pevensies' watch the wardrobe click shut.

Fur coated glory matted, gasoline drenched and swiftly crisped,
Ashen halos falling, falling in Autumn's coming,

and the Great Lion, and all his mighty heart,
Lay still.

Adara (With help from Not a Muse)

My daughter's story begins with "Once Upon a Time..."

For two years my pen lingered around her silhouette,
Cursor marking tick and tock, reticent

When she was the bun and I was the baker,
In a tome, tummy in hand, I chronicled her father and brother,
So I've taken those leaves and lay them a dozen
My little shape-shifter, my loaf, look how you've risen.

Keeper of Memory,
Remember the anecdotes, and hold tight when they ring true,
Take the guilt with a pinch of salt for every sin you accrue,

Freedom Fighter,
Knit yourself closely to your own truth,
Take it from mama, you don't have to make any excuses for youth,

Keeper of Secrets
There is no weakness in admitting wrong,
Descendant of two moors, your blood is primed to beat strong,

Archetype
Resolutions are simple, if you simply choose what you love,
Govern by your own morality, regardless of what name you call to above,

Creator
Effort is a precondition,
Without it you undermine all your conviction,

Landscaper
Your body is a means - not a definition,
Subjecting yourself to derision is a decision,

Home-maker
Pain will clutch, with its many tentacles around brain, heart and gut,
There is no answer for loss, no contentment in "Just Because"

Lover
You should not need to question love.

Myth Maker
The universe owes us nothing, but do not hold yourself to this,
Creation trumps consumption, idleness, hardly worth the risk,

Explorer
May your gaze face outward and continue to guzzle,
I caution only to make passion your goal, not your prison,

Daughter
Regret only a cold cup of tea,
Commit the rest to muscle memory.

Your curls have lengthened, and in my eyes,
Your shadow brings shame to sunlight,
I have given you the beginning to your story,
A start, a syllable, a cursor, a cue,
And I've known what to pass on, because of you.

Not A Muse is a 2009 poetry anthology.

Free Verse

Do you know it took two outfit changes to get here?
In the morning when time is a necklace with a stubborn clasp,
At the pause between the doorway,
I leave my novel and promises of bedtime,
Both too big for my laptop bag.

Does she see the forehead crease,
Eyes that dart from computer to playmat,
Pause. Peekaboo! Slackens -
And the phone rings.

Textbooks balanced on eggshells.
I studied until birdsong last night,
We're at dinner. Do they know about the ballpoint stains on my finger?
Sipping water teaspoons at a time, conversation trickles into a gush,
to the final "*This was fun, we'll do this again soon.*"

This poem has love handles to trim,
So I use free-verse like a little black dress,
To cover the child at my breast,
Pacify the academic at rest,
Between signatures and meetings,
When sleep is fleeting,

For every stanza unwritten,
So this time does not fade into the forgotten.

Semantic Satiation

Tap tap cursor on this screen,
Clicks on my tongue where your name used to be,

Now you're both the fore and shadow,
Exposition turned prophecy.

Let's tamper with the cartography of memory,
Untangle weights of meaning from songs and jokes,

Forge Rosaline's out of Juliet,
Remove details like Romeo, and set this story free.

I think of Count Paris sometimes,
Another mislaid plan in someone else's life,

I think he had it best of all.

Truth is, no straw could break a back as well as a knife,
And we both felt a prick of relief twisting -
Between our shoulder blades that night.

My mouth gapes around your name, still too easy to say.
You became a poem I could not write,
A fullstop I can't place

Reed Wrought Worlds

Life synonymised,
A pen conscripted to devise,
Draw the line between affliction and compulsion,

An itch to craft, curate, or simply relate.
In five to ten minutes, to possibly hate.
I write to be certain I was really awake.

Words on a page, networking a neural blaze,
Each flip, a visceral oar dip,
Into a river whose pebbled borders are adorned with poetry,

Underneath, worlds lie larger than Atlantis
Stories, fragments and letters to fidget with,
All water may lead to the sea, but I am left thirsty.

For a few moments at least,
It leaves a handy pebbled trail,
To an astonishingly long exhale,

Or, a way to cope with my white whale.

Tai O Village

History for them is like ginger,
Built over the exposed film
Of thousands of lives, lived afloat
Before and after their time.
The storm grinds and they make
Thunder inside with their mahjong tiles,
We three still slower than we need be, strolling past
The irony of dried fish hanging in the rain,

Patrolling crabs amongst the mangrove dwarfs,
Shying as first rain falls, like
Long-legged grasshoppers in the wind,
There are squeals and thuds for shelter,
The damp wood squeaks,
On pebbled paths,
Slippers slap past
Coats darken from the damp,

My boy has fallen asleep inside the buggy
Trapped air warming his soft skin,
Away from life's curiosities for now,
Wet stares, shrines hydrant-red as we stalk past,
The storm grinds and they watch
From Inside the hollows of their homes,
We're caught in a spectator sport,
Somewhere between sodden and soaked,
Framed through a window.

Diary of an Expat Immigrant

Home is a four-letter word.
You're supposed to know what it means.
Say it with confidence.
So the other kids know,
You know.
You Know?

I've introduced myself in front of enough classes,
To know what they expected me to say,
How to say it,
With a lilt,
A rounded R,
Or an emphasis that trails...

As an adult; they say I keep my voice heard,
Under oceans and over mountains,
Phone lines, like my accent, roaming.

I pledge allegiance to no flag,
They signify anthropology more than nationality,

No political party to get under my skin,
Or a need to call for blood,
Veterans to admire but few to thank,

Only with sports do I take sides,
During wars, I get to straddle the line.
And that was all fine.

Until I wondered how fresh soil would feel that was all mine,
To clench my fist and breathe the musk of,
A part of the earth that would grow a bloodline.

For home to be a place, not a story.

But home is a four-letter word,
Built on ideas about belonging.
Specifically, about who belongs, and
Who should come, and who should keep going.

I would rather no box to tick,
Hate to borrow, or inherit,
Can't feel hard done by what was not yours,
You can't be abandoned by a story,

So home is a four-letter word,
My tale is footfalls oceans and mountains long,
The world remains supported by a ring of elephants
on the back of a tortoise,

So wherever you are,
And wherever you go,
you're already home.

Last Day of Summer at the Beach

I don't need a poem to remember this day.
So I will only say,
Fearlessness is her little body,
Amongst the waves, limbs flaying in delight.
His reluctance morphing into joy,
I will struggle to articulate for every crossroad I know of in his life.

Salty air can taste like taffy,
Draped around you in the sticky sweet joy of summer.
The horizon will remind you more than pictures from Mars of your smallness,
You will want to tangle your insignificance in it.
Become a giant rubber band ball of worries bounced against the line,
Which marks sea from sky.
A squash game, all reflexes and no wrist,
Clumsy stumbles on crag
Feel the crush of shells on your wet, raisined toes, that you don't mind
because -
There is joy in running to it, to give it a good solid, thwack.

When I think about that day,
I remember how I felt their easiness ebb and flow as though they were still
inside me.
In fearlessness, a promise.
In the ability to find joy, peace of mind.

And the horizon, quite simply, taught me,
Where to draw the line.

stage steɪdʒ/

noun

2.

a raised floor or platform, typically in a theatre, on which actors, entertainers, or speakers perform.

synonyms: platform, dais, stand, grandstand, staging, apron, rostrum, podium, soapbox, stump;

STAGE II

The girl plays tetris for the most part

The trouble was not who I was,
It was how I was going to be
All of it,
Without knowing if any of it,
Was truly me.

Accent

My accent roves
from page to stage,
To stages and teachers,
and apples not eaten,
Good eggs and bad ones,
Conference calls and grocery runs,
Enunciate, premeditate,
Settles with the other nomads.

End of the World

"Is there anything worse than spilled coffee?"
My colleague groaned as wads of paper towel,
Seeped more resin than bean.

"Crying over it" I responded.
"That's worse,
After all, it's not the end of the world."

This memory is strange to where I sit, back straight,
Tissue in hand, wearing my favourite dress;
(mid-length black 50s throwback with white accents)
— the only thing I have in funeral-black resplendence.

It's not the end of the World, I thought again on December 21st,
But I've watched as some worlds fell away,
And took with them the words to carve out the fall,
All I've got is all cloy and no taste, a burn on my tongue.

Grief lacks context to a child's mind,
That death falls short of definition, my love, is death defined,
Just like that, you the space becomes a place inside those you leave behind,
A pulse in the quiet, where arteries don't quicken.

Tell a child of a void and they will want to fill it -
I'll draw you a picture, stop crying, mama - that's enough.
After all, it's not the end of the world,
You've said it before,
Crying over spills,
Won't change anything,

December 21st 2011 did not bring on the end of the world, as projected by Mayan prophecy.

A year has passed,
Inseparable to the last,
Two coffins,
Side by side, lacquered white,
Impossibly small.
Bouquets with notes loving, better suited
for blue icing on cake, laughter spilling from open doorways where muddy
rugby boots linger.

I won't forget,
Their boyish grins,
Their parents who remain,
All kindness and grace,
Who continue with pace, and priority,
Where there is simply no place for cheap coffee.

First Light

My first memory of writing is a veneer wooden table,
Ballpoint blue making jagged letter-shapes,
'Bun' 'cat' 'a-b-d-c',
They did not need words to mean anything,

Fan-blades click with each rotation,
In a bright tropical light, letters reveled, fuzzed and sharpened
the *whip whip* blades adding to the fantastical
baila of memory.

When I was a child, the smallest push made a thought free-fall into an idea,
Constellations did not ask for their stars to be joined,
And without anybody's permission, that four year old befriended her mind.

That was my first stumble into magic.
The second happened a few weeks ago,

My four year old's homework comes in dot-dot-dot's, trace the letter,
Strokes one, two, three - always, one, two, three.
Use a ruler to join the sound and the picture.
Colour her dress red, no, not blue, Red.
There are lines, that he must stay in - not straddle,
His letters must sit,
And if his pencil is not sharp enough we get notes sent home.

See that, I *still* get notes sent home.

At bedtime he takes the book from me,
And we're back there again - the world about to get bigger,
The hover before a first step,

Baila is Sri Lankan folk genre.

He reads the shape, his lips rhythmic, lashes flick
from print to glossy oxford reader pictures for a hint,
He finds cliffhangers in the sound of a suffix,
his voice mounting to hysteria, look at me, mummy!
Our grins playing Marco Polo,

My boy has already found a way outside the lines,
Eyes glistening with first dew of new sight.

Uprooted

Roots threadlike and sallow, curled, shy from the sun.
The tug of wind,
Make them sway flaccid in all directions,

They place me in new soil,
Do not look at me in my newness,
They place me in new soil,
Burlap gloves scratch, then sear.
Where am I?
The kiss of nitrogen poured neat,
Where are you?
It ebbs to a pulse,
A whisper,
A *phantom longing*,
You, are a phantom longing.
And mama said there are no such things as ghosts.

25 Year Divorce

"I've moved on" she says at the twitch of inquiry,
The words fall from her lips neatly parted,
crisp of parting's posterity,
She tries them on for size,
Soon, they will naturalize.

The leaf is turned and she looks down at the sheet,
staunched, ironed, bare,
Letters printed with the greatest care,
Her name glistening in inked resignation.

Her rubix cube identity,
Twists to her new home past Mrs to Ms,
Chants like an incantation,
To harden a heart so golden,
but tarnished by years, silvered, and harnessed in the past.
Time spent under his paperweight, snowed in as
Dry-ice memory outlasts its chill.

Sure you've seen it before - but it's sadder than you think,

She took for granted the coming of an expiry date,
Her purpose marked her poise
When she used to shout, but now what about?

But my, how she smiles,
Like a break in the frost,
Her secret has been her strength,
Under that ocean lay her 98%.

Something Borrowed

An artist shot a video of two strangers kissing for the first time,
Bodies in coy shapes,
Tiptoeing around a pregnant space,
Between them clammy, static anticipation.

That's when the video buffered.
Reduced to pixels with cold feet,
Before open lips, an embrace, the close of skin, time, and space.
At the very tip of the very best bit.

Would it have stopped there.
Expectation mounted heavy in the air,
Then left at the alter.
Like steam clearing from your glasses,
When you leave a hot room, for a cold one.

In the Woods

A couple of clicks,
For a friend to turn stranger,
Significant, as a tree falling in a lonely forest.

Well, it makes a sound,
In case you were wondering,
and my friend has been taken deep.

She's an upstart. Foreign,
Hair billowing, vine-like, around him,
Her prospects glimmer, dew on a dream catcher,
Gives him enough rope to hang himself with.

I'm left a little annoyed,
but it's my Wild Thing
against his Medusa,
I don't want to turn into cold stone,

I rather ruckus and roar with those who care,
Work on laughter lines and conversation
Without reserve or condescension
Over supper, which is invariably, always, hot.

This poem references children's book *Where The Wild Things Are* by Maurice Sendak.

From My Table

Why do flowers smell their sweetest, just before they die?
Petals thin and fall in clumps,
Worshipping at the altar of greying stems.

In my grandmother's garden, pebbles scattered,
Startled by the applause of rubber slippers running to iron swings,
Rusty and screaming - as higher and higher - my feet dangling wild,
Like falling stems over a vase,

All I could smell was the red of those flowers on the branches above,
We would pluck them, one by one and suck on their nectar,
Before they fell and were spoilt.

Years later I married an Irishman who told me stories of the 'sweet smell' of a
rotting harvest,
Famine, swift and indiscriminate.

I spoke to a man the other day, He said;
'I went to your country and you should thank your lucky stars to be where
you are.
He told me everything was dirty there; the buses, the streets, the people, the
money,
He told me tales he heard of children forced to shoot their parents,
and hate so palpable, it stung your nose.'

A time before I was born,
My father walked past the swing in that same garden,
Past the lane he saw his neighbour's - head, on a stake outside his home.

I was told this, years later in an impassioned tone,
Sometimes things just happen, and that's all we are to ever know.

Suffering does not compromise,
If nothing else, the greatest honour for a parent is to give life twice,
Theirs did, and so did mine -
Except, all we had to do was board a flight.

I pluck the flowers from my vase, one at a time.
As my children play around me,
We will visit soon, a month or so away,
But will it smell the same, when we arrive?

Winter's Song

The violinist is Jack Frost tonight.
City kaleidoscoped in the underpass,
Chatter echoes around curved walls,
Snowflakes decaled vertically on string,
Fairy lights sway heavily in the wind.

Sound falls away to footsteps, Jack, string and bow.
The song starts soft and slow, stretching now to then,
Rooted in the middle of a municipal blend,
All is dark, just me and him -
Standing lulled, mulled by dregs from the past flavouring the present.

How are they to know that I am dry drowning? -
Breath shortened by the thwang of a violin,
Slipped between the pruning skin of ice and frigid water,
Brought in by splashes of something from before,
Taking me further and further from tomorrow.

Sudden as when you rub your hands against the cold,
The chill wears off, the noises rush back, all car-honks and babies crying,
Buildings adorned luminescent by thousands of bulbs, We see
Dasher and Dancer Prance upon Vixen,
Comet has run away with Cupid all-aDonner in the Blixen,

The faraway dong of the clocktower, rings in the back
like sleigh bells, trilling into adulthood,
Soft and slow,
Jack and his bow,
Dasher and Dancer all aglow,

I turn to re-join the masses, holding a candle in my mind,
The wick will grow small, the wax will seep,
The journey will trudge along its intended path
But the memories are what I keep,
Selected carefully to bauble a sprawling fir tree.

Sometimes the Rabbit Hole

Sometimes the rabbit hole,
Starts in your ear canal,
Coloured fragments dance
Like particles in the wind,
A psycho-delic leak of techno-media seep,
Eyebags burning -
With the weight of
the whole world gone to shit
With
#FirstWorldProblems

Other days, there are Sunday nights without a 9PM stomach drop
No it's *hump day* reassurances,
Or *Friday I'm in Love* euphoria,

Time is not tied to a clock,
No saline drip-drop sting of morning's first kiss.
The lift doors open when they should,
I remember to do the voices at story time,
And taste my coffee.

The leaves don't fall here in autumn,
I crave assurances of a half-season,
The crunch under balls of feet,
A sign that as things change, they will do so again.
And sanity is just a catherine wheel,
a rabbit hole,
a state of play.

Lily

You feel like a lily in a flower press,
Veins track marks to where life entered and left the door open,
Entwining your person in long and latitudinal whispers from pubic bone to temple,
Blood carries the shock, babbling from spleen to breastbone,
Forearms draw tight to trap it somewhere in your chest,
A stubborn little clot you are certain the world can see through your paper-thin skin.

You'll tell a few friends over the years,
Carefully or matter of fact,
All the while probing from your eyes to the shocked O of their mouths,
They can't believe that bad things happen to good people,
You can't believe it doesn't show.

Some days it feels like a pacemaker keeping you in check,
Padding an extra layer between you and the world,

Other days it retreats behind a scab, shiny sinew and muscle tissue,
"It's that numb bit, press it at hard as you want, I feel nothing."

The worst are the casual flickers that reveal a world a page turn away,
Where the lily can tumble out, brittle, and aged,

But the book your grandma sleeps with had one thing right,
Blood will wash, swill and spit,
Skin layers and folds around you,
But are only part of the sum of what lies inside,
Though some of those parts hollowed you while you tried,

One day you walk beyond coping,
Inventorying your body,
and just keep going.

Courage

"The ability to do something that frightens one."
From the Latin 'coeur' meaning heart.
To function when synapses spark to parts best left in the dark.
Leave,
Stay,
Make the most of it,
Run away.

Renounce the boogie man,
Take the high road in your head,
Banish the monsters under your bed.
To carpe your diem,
To fumble your 'mea culpa'
To howl,
To roar,

It is to take,
To spare,
To cope,
"The ability to do something that frightens one."
- in the absence of hope.

But you won't find that in a dictionary.

I'm Looking for a Word

I fell asleep with a mental straight-jacket on,
Words dripping like the bathroom tap
lapping tongue of my cat, too fat
and to be honest a bit of a sociopath.

I have trails of thought running to catch the last train,
It's that feeling of walking into a room and forgetting what you were ...
This word I'm looking for to say the important thing,
But simpler,
With line breaks —

It's a compulsion for ... *something*
A propensity with a hint of insert word here
I am in the sensory deprivation tank before an affirmative nod,
A blinking cursor too closely attributed to writer's block.

There might be a word for it in another language,
But I'm struggling with this one let alone two,
I need a word-like crowbar to jack open,
band-aid-rip,
hard consonants to hit you like ... *thingy*

I want to be eight again.
Gargle words as part of my nightly routine,
chew softly lolling them round,
lick with satisfaction the menthol on my lips,

I'd weave daisy chains out of synonyms and antonyms,
Played jump rope with those hard to say,
like seeds from a pomegranate, do you bite through or just
let it linger to a stain?

I collected notebooks like stamps,
And unfinished stories I'd call stumps,
As though to sit on
in a clearing with unruly leaves,
muted birds, and a sober sun,
Waiting for a friend to come along.

Airborne

The horizon is a smear of yolk inside a robin's egg,
This is the best way to see it, floating in the albumen,
Cabin pressure tightens my temple,
Ears block, thoughts more private,
Out the window, Sun ray splotches float green and gold,
The plane's wing, a toast soldier dunking in a soft-boiled sunrise.

'Oh God' hundreds chorused when our plane slumped,
Pitch perfect, a clamour of voices,
An empty drop in my heart,
Or my stomach
Or from heart to stomach
Perennial suspension,
When there is no missing step,
you sent the wrong email,
or your child goes missing at the supermarket.

Buttery oxygen masks fall out,
Tendril-like sways,
Time sputtered,
Suddenly raced,
when the plane swerved stable,

The masks like sad limp condoms hang,
Twisting in the sun,
A small giggle breaks my lips
And my ears pop with the dawn.

New Year's Eve

At the office by chance,
At night, the buildings below stick out at odd angles,
The many jagged teeth of The Man, laughing.

The fish dawdle in their tank,
Papers stacked, in hurried farewells,
Amongst empty boxes of Christmas chocolate, marooned wine glasses,
The darkness drinks me in,

The plant on my desk, young, snake green,
That thrives despite a fluorescent sun,
Had slumped,
Leaves spayed,
Hands up - had enough.

I tip in an offering, using a small canary yellow can,
It bit against the dark, hard, like daylight,
and made my eyes, ring, then quiver for the rest of the night.

I came back on the third of January,
The green lustered, stood proud, restored to its former vitality,
Something smug, you know, for a plant -
Something like an augury.

STAGE II

The girl noises her voice

She acquiesced the voice was hers,
Though thinned and dulled when played back.

Could count like rings on a tree,
From branch to sapling to seed,

Where life thickened her words
And didn't even leave a mark.

The Aged Expats

The years they estimated in inches,
Stretched and spooled into centimetres,

Sun-lines and freckles on skin,
Folded as the local newspaper on his lap,

She blows on her jasmine or chrysanthemum tea,
Cupping it close, as red lanterns dance above her head,

They chew the fat with wafts of shrimp paste in the air,
Sampans gently knocking against the dock,

Casually tethered,
Ready to go,

Which is likely why they stay.

A Love Poem

I want to write a poem for you that would look dreadful on paper,
I've written these lines, a handful a day at a time, like plucking flowers on a
walk for our table.
I'll arrange them haphazardly,
Half-talking about my day,
My hands rifling through the mundane,
Shuffling papers, wiping crumbs,
Echoes of our lives scattered like sweets wrappers -
(That in a less sentimental mood would have me enraged)

I like how you know to leave me in my tundras,
Let the stillness blizzard over me.
Know that I will lose sleep day-dreaming,
That I will take my neuroses out for a run and we'll come back with ideas,
And you ready to take the baton,

I love how you rub your hands, blow into them and cup mine,
You do this as though lighting a candle,
So the warmth spreads red hot,

Then there are times my nerves fill with frost,
You know well the sound of a sniff in the pause where my finger circles the
buttons to push.
Get the hairs on your back to stand straight,
Bite the words that would cut creases into your forehead,
Angrily stalk to the sofa eyes like poisoned darts,
Your words blunt, mine sharp,

I can be missish too, and petty, and affectatious and a little bit the fool,
Raise a scornful eyebrow at the pretty waitress,
Somewhere between pity and knowing I've never been much for sharing,
I'll turn green and you'll laugh at me
and eke out a smile from the venom.

You still try to talk about things I've given you no reason to ever suppose I'd
be interested in,
I've heard that story before, you know,
But I'll hear it again, and I will do my best to listen,
Because we both know it takes much more than to have and to hold,
That you give life to more than kids, pets, and a home.
This thing sanctified by
God
Or
Paper
Or
Memory lives on.
Asks to be
fedwateredpruned
then left alone.
Be cupped between warm hands,
as though lighting a candle,
so the warmth spreads red hot.
And that's why this is a love poem,
because it could have just as easily have been not.

Siu Ap Fan with a Visitor

"What was it like to grow up in Hong Kong?"
"Do you speak Cantonese?"
Sometimes, it was like living in the waiting room of an airport.
And like in the airport, everything is translated three times,
So no, I don't speak Cantonese.

I tell her, I am my own brand of local;
The kind that doesn't carry an umbrella with me.
Come 6 o'clock my contact lenses feel like peanut brittle.
I too, am an MTR test-tube baby; earphones umbilical to device that lets me recline fetal in my mind.
I have the right to land and an accent that won't settle.

We are in line for *Siu Ap Fan*,
Realizing too late, this was not a meal for two.
All that bone spitting and rice shoveling,
It's for sinewy fragments-in-your-teeth kind of thinking.
Fat sizzles on crispy duck skin and runs down your chin,
We slurp and gnaw and revel, all teeth and no conversation.

The duck man's lunch grind requires a strut that is;
Part mother hen, part factory supervisor,
A furrowed brow, cleaver
Heave-ho'ing,
Clang-bang people traffic, an instant spill into the streets like
a fresh teabag in water. B*o le* slammed down next to me, chopsticks
rattle, and a plus on my ticket tells them to call order six
Not *lok*.
My duck man knows how to cater to those like me.

She asks about sovereignty.
I talk about the trees on Hollywood road, branches procumbent,
Snaking like varicose veins on the island's asphalt skin,
Money pumped into mountains scraped back,
Only to have its soil entailed to northern cousins.
Sometimes it takes a little ingenuity,
To build bricks out of a make believe place,
Like a plus on a ticket,
A white bauhinia amongst the red,
Because you see, Hong Kong, like me
is a third culture kid who writes her own story.

Siu ap fan is Cantonese for "Chinese BBQ duck with rice". B*o le* is a type of tea. L*ok* is Cantonese for "six". "Procumbent" is a botanical term: (of a plant or stem) growing along the ground without throwing out roots.

The Orchard

My daughter pointed out the giraffe first.
Her cheek hot, splat against the metal frame of the window,

My son reasoned it was a diplodocus-
It's elongated neck exaggerated, upwards.

I saw a *kayan lahwi,*
Yellow struck brass by the sun.

The bus passes the construction yard,
We three, rattling at the front
Apples from the same tree.

Kayan lahwi are Myanmar women who wear brass neck coils.

Twilight Years

The sun splinters,
Walking through town's mid-day glare,
An assembly of hawk-jarring eyes,
Hair-peeling-from-skull wiles,
Floral patterns dulled by the light,
pasted on curved spines,
Sag on jaundice-glow skin,
Ligaments lax, still as mountains,
Eyes - old, stagnant, cold.

On the walkway where buskers hang on top of roads
An old woman stands alone, condoned,
Hawks weary resignation, at the
hand of law's inferiority complex,
He reaps her charge,
Broken zip agape on frayed coin pouch,
It makes my face, as hers looks as though she lost
whatever piece she held onto.

They say these people always fall,
if only it were my call.

I pause for -
Spit-laced words fade to a far ...
Cobbled, concrete seat
I see this member of the enforcement of peace,
Amongst the discontented,
Twilight years, gout-swollen-face, burnt-bitter tobacco
Desecrated,
Discarded,
Old, stagnant and cold.

Golem

It happens to a piece of clay as it warms.
Takes form.
A crack,
A careless nail print,
Then a lattice of hairline fractures,
Perhaps foreshadowing a future break.

You can fill the fissures with more of the same,
Prepare the structure for strain,
But I am made of flesh, not clay.

Minibus

I told my son
You've got to lean into the turns
Or leave yourself open to be sent off-kilter

Your daddy can tell you how the physics works,
Your mama will tell you that's how life is.

Newspaper Woman

I've lined my stall with world news and anime porn,
Darkened with rain and pollution,
Corners blunted and bent by harried passers-by -
Doggy-eared in submission to their phones.

I am pitied only by librarians,
The ringmaster nods collegiate,
Knows the costs of running the show beyond the cover price,
Newsprint so fresh it tattoos fish and chips,
Burns hot, the stories that
give voice to telegraphs, anonymous tips,
astigmatism and carpel tunnel,
The pomp, the nasal, the vitriolic.

Then a pound became a penny,
Headlines baited,
And you bit.
Clicked,
And clicked.
The Glock locked,
Silencer in place,
Click.

When banks became smoking mirrors, children washed ashore,
You rallied around hashtags, but I don't see you anymore,
The horrors echoed farther, women silenced, hospitals bombed,
Distant from the blue afterglow on your skin,
Their nameless faces and faceless names all-but-never lived.

Go ahead and blame the papers,
As you tap out your outrage,
Look unto your newsfeed, ignore the front page,
The thing that may be awkward for you to now find,
They bit,
They writ.
When it was you that didn't click.

Zeitgeist

Reads like a history book doesn't it?
Like that time Mr. Harvey spoke to us about sex.
Our backs straightened in interest,
Polyester mix uniforms sticking in the late August humidity,

Source
Example
Explanation

We'd annotate source A
And source B
Our yellow pencils
Ring fencing the obvious
In circular tuts,
You're telling me they couldn't see it coming?
Facts stubborn as we were.

Forgive me for being generation Sesame street.
Raised on Michael Jackson-pollocked vision of life with my technicolour friends,
Surrounded by all the languages we spoke and the food we shared,
Tables that just got longer as we grew,

A hard fought reality,
The human salve after centuries of being bound by the ropes of intolerance,
Assured of the hairline cracks we'd add to that glass ceiling,
Of the equitable men these boys promised to grow into,
A conviction that we were on the right side of history.

Less than two decades later,
I'd be sitting at a dinner party,
Slowly twisting the napkin in my lap,
Elbows cramped, navigating a small dim-lit table,
Listening to -
It's nothing to do with us ...
... people need to calm down ...
this is what happens when you hand out awards for participation ...

Except this is the reaction -
From those who participate.
Who bear witness,
Who say not in my name,
Who'll ride with you,
Who expect better.

Pixels jar from the news screen,
A living embodiment of democracy,
Not broken, just doing its job - exposing the blackheads.
Suddenly surfaced in an angry digital smear.
Virulent. Pumped through airwaves, and satellites,
In shores across the world,

People detained for having a certain last name,
Or stacked as though already dead in jail,
Shot clean through the head for how their skin looks against the night,
Turning away those who run to water, when land burns their heels.
Things reported but remain unclicked.
Because Baghdad and Pakistan have had their 15 minutes,
As have the Uighurs and Rohingyas, Naru, and Darfur,
Syria, Palestine, and a list as deep as a lake that no longer ripples,

These are problems for other people.
Sow fear and ignorance; yield a bad crop.
Bellies torched with fire,
Stoking the idea of famine and a hunger for Justice.

(It's nothing to do with her either.)
Blindfolded, her scales long rigged,
Rusted still with generations of blood lust,

Mr. H would laugh at me, and say with history comes clarity,
With the lack of clarity comes choice
To be a listener or to be the voice.

I've heard this before, as have you
These desperate times the source of discontent,
Perhaps it's for us to be the example,
So we can one day explain,
That when the time came, we the many acted on behalf of the few,
Because nothing will change
Unless we want it to.

Masquerade

I can see it when you smile,
A quiver under your eye,
Tectonic worries.
A trembling cliff, overlooking rolling, dark hills.

Have you ever wondered if this was it?
Superhero mask formed in the bags under your eyes,
Anxiety caped around your torso,
Your body a host for its pangs and whims.

When you jolt awake at night, sweat flanneled to your skin,
Do you gasp out of relief or surprise,
That you aren't Icarus,
That isn't hot wax down your side,

You wonder how long before you fall,
At the supermarket,
Post office or caught between train doors,

You know all this,
Your greatest strength,
Bound by its consequence,

Like Prometheus lighting a spliff,
Waiting for the eagle to arrive.

Chronicle

We would not look remiss in an Escher sketch,
Pavements slant,
Buildings perch,
Jutting like a witch's smile,
Human gridlock,
Leading tetris-block lives,

Humidity like a shroud, bursting with
beads of perspiration on pricked raw skin.
The type of hot that bursts out of a *har gau* dumpling
that make sweat draw lines down your back.

Cement slapped on like after-thoughts,
We walk with hands in pockets, or clutching a strap,
Our seams stitched twice, so our jingle-jangle beliefs don't fall out,
In the bustle of wet street corners,
Fallen coins,
Torn flyers,
Oil splashed from *siu mai* vendors,
Drainage covers stampeded into roads,
Sealing lost tunnels where our feet reverberate
Thousands of lifelines,
Written in ghost-hand by the city.

It scribes on rock, brick and earth,
dented, eroded, poisoned and tagged,
unearthed, silt slips giving way
to landslides, failing mountains forming steps we climb.
Trails we walk, choppy waters we float on,
We take the road less travelled, the roads we speak of,
later when memory selects, edits, portrays,

But, you know, the pavement does not change,
The patterns remain,
Railings rust as we walk,
Beaches crumble as we lie,
Stories imprints with each passing,
Tales of 7 million and the many before
in neat cryptography pens invisible birthmarks
and eulogies.

Moral Dyslexia

Can I be honest with you?
Inquired the proverbial book.
I know not where a sentence may end,
Look – Ink was all it took.

Flesh out my pulp and soon you'll find,
Just how readily fibers unwind,
Ideas have evolved from thread, to sheet,
To funeral shroud,

I am the soundless lackey,
Arsenal to emotions they cannot govern without.
Go pluck from the flotsam of the Holy land,
A stick to sketch their border with,
Let their pounds of flesh be claimed,
And their blood spilt freely like sand,

Their infants small and crumpled
on heaving breasts, full and engorged with milk,
When my teachings lie dismembered as their limbs,
When their bodies lie cold in the sun,
They will know it was not by Us they acted upon.

But Book, what of the World
That follows with morbid fascination,
To the tune of self-righteous recitation,
These words are shrapnel in disguise,
Aimed to pierce the place between the eyes,

And Book you drag my eyes apart,
There is a dull ache in the temple,
A clot of fear in my heart,
The cold mosque stone echo;
Allahu Akbar
With gritted teeth you know they strain to say
"God is great, this blessed strife
Is an all-absolving sacrifice."

And I suppose you'll say they're right,
For those whose only option is the after-life.
And you know as well as I,
This war is not divine,
This is a question of identity,

Of self-preservation, of human degradation,
Look at the promise of their wily condemnation,
Conspiracy leached from your tome,
Debris amongst the bones, that lie in your name,
Of which moral dyslexia is all they can ever claim.

Yellow Umbrella

I like stories for the young,
They are a three-course meal,
A beginning, middle and end.
Loose-bits tied,
A reader satisfied.
Narratives that gain momentum,
Cavort exposition,
Hits a nerve,
Hooks your navel,
Until a full-stop, snap-bang, loud, and final.

Gluttons for information behind a screen,
Skim words and bite to test the realness as though of a coin.
News becomes a loop of static noise,
We untangle wires, lament how
It all turns to vinegar so soon after the first sip of wine,

These past few weeks,
When like angry bees in black and yellow they took to the streets,
Long poles on their shoulders, they carry my children's future wrapped in a handkerchief.
Where the fuck was Mary Poppins then?
Open Sesame - Ali Baba, they brought the commercial sector to its feet,
And still no Robin Hood appeared,
Hansel forgot to lay the bread-crumbs out of here,
This is no bed-time story.

The bells in limbo have begun,
The ground will soon disappear.
You can add oil to a slippery slope,
But it only serves the fall that is near.

These are not the lost kids of never-land,
They are not idealistic to demand,
No pounds of flesh exchanged for a square foot of land,
A vote that counts, that doesn't just tally,

I walked among them, for an hour,
Cardboard signs and voices hoarse but they rally
"be careful"
"ga yau"
"pick up your rubbish"
"ga yau"
"if not now, then when?"
"ga yau'
And now I watch the plot unravel,
Behind my screen, torn but not quite in between.
But it's hit a nerve,
Hooked my navel.

These are stories of the young.
It will have a beginning, middle and an end,
Gain momentum
Cavort exposition

These are the stories of the young
These are the tales of what we'll all become.

Ga yau is Cantonese for "Add Oil", a term of encouragement.

The Leap

It's very matter of fact you know,
It's a long way down from the top.

In a vertical city,
They leap, they fly.

They torpedo,
They glide.

A young man jumped off the building due to emotional stress,
A woman in her thirties was distressed,
A 90 year old man jumped because his heart was broken,
A man jumped off a building out of frustration,

An entrepreneur
A mixed girl
An expatriate
A korean woman
An indonesian beautician
A devoted mother
Somebody's child, somebody's brother.

Published on a property website,
As though a torn scrap from an obituary,
A caution for the living.

I've known one who flew,
It took me years to understand that trying to live left him breathless,
I think about the ways we fall,
in love
into debt
out with someone
down a black hole.
Not ever really meaning to.

I never found out if he left a note behind,
Just a wife and a child.

We never knew of the sadness that plagued him,
Like a cancer grew, and now that sound of silence
rings louder than the friend I knew.

The list grows tall as the city,
As we balk at the violence,
Yet feed its gilded belly, with jumpers offered as rent.

Property websites in Hong Kong publicly disclose the manner in which previous tenants have died.

The Entrepreneur's Song

In the end we all become story-tellers.
Passed from song to palm,
From the batik print of a life-line to wall art,
The clatter of print blocks,
to binary love notes.

Except we tell them all wrong.
Sidle past the seven dwarfs -
Gave Snow White a castle, a soundtrack,
and a reality tv show,

We dress Innovation in the halogen glow of a city,
Home it with chandeliers, the red twinkle of a plane against a navy night,
Reserve its stories for the haughty, the enigmatic, the eccentric and
intellectual,
Thump it on the back, call it a cousin of evolution.

Beyond nanotech, Palo Alto
Fibre optics, the distant whirr of drones,
It lies with bits and bytes thrown into the bin on a desktop,
Left crumpled on the cutting room floor,

A drip at the end of a parched tap,
WD-40 to the mind's nuts and bolts,
In leathered hands that lay bricks, colour pencil scrawls on the wall,
In spent chalk dust thick enough to leave footprints,
In chapped fingers and coffee grounds.

At times best seen from a slow shutter speed,
to sharpen nuances, and equalize the light,
A narrative that stretches beyond the first act,
Finding a story halfway to the end,
and capturing the courage to being again.

A dream that becomes a face tick,
A side stitch,
A piece of bread, hot and doughy in the middle
to feed a modest revolution,

It is stitching rocks in your belly
- Making do -
Rubbing sticks together and praying it will spark,
It is running on empty but still taking part.

Taken With a Pinch of Salt

If I had known about my life, I would have asked for a trigger warning.
Or at least a parental advisory sticker.
I received neither, much less $200 when I passed Go,

I couldn't predict my own knack of getting in my way,
Face forward to the moon, hollering for my shadow,
I turn around, only for the bastard to trip me up.

The mind a sandstorm of chemicals
siphoned into a respiratory function I call 'making do'
One step after the other,
Frog-marched me from pillow to bus stop,

I thought with my brain,
Felt with my heart,
- and never once did I let them cross paths.

Except, all the time because variety is the spice of life
Half the fun, unpicking truth from idiom,
Sporting mistakes like hickeys, bruises, and if persistent, tattoos.

They couldn't have told me how black holes suck from within,
Hope whittled down and quivering in your marrow,
We are, after all, the stuff of stardust,
At times your small pieces of universe threaten collapse,

They call me Wonder Woman
But really, I'm more Incredible Hulk
Frustration pins my stasis,
No brawn could move mountains like resolve,

Or so the stubborn say, when stubborn is your resume.

They say, that's all fine, but look at how well you've done -
I'd like a piece of your energy, manufactured into pills
Or attach as puppet strings to auto-pilot the day.

At what price, I always mean to say -
Because another idiom is be careful what you wish for,

Chase dopamine to loosen a cortisol grip on life,
Crave melatonin most days, and ignore it most nights.
Whole weeks it goes in circles and times it fades to black.

It doesn't matter,
I know better,
I put one foot in front of the other.

Acknowledgements

First to David McKirdy and Peter Gordon at Chameleon Press for their excellent guidance and stewardship. Next to my fellow poets at Peel Street Poetry from across the years who are hopefully still writing ferociously wherever in the world they may now be; this community is an enduring source of inspiration and to whom I owe a deep debt of gratitude. Special thanks to Keith McMullen—without whose spark and keen sense of mischief, we may have never met on a Wednesday to read a few poems all those years ago. To my co-directors, Henrik Hoeg and Akin Jeje, two of the finest poets and friends one could hope to have, thank you both for your generous spirit, banter and unwavering encouragement.

To my fellow Hong Kong poets, both at Peel Street Poetry and Outloud you are too numerous to name, I have included you by omission. Your influence has been far-reaching, and has made up most of my writing life. Your words are indelible—whether in gobbledygook, about watching football down the pub, orations of justice and equality, in sonnet form, about birds, dragons, humans, werewolves, and so on.

To my family, in Hong Kong, Sri Lanka, Australia, the UK, and scattered across the world, thank you for your humour, your stories and love.

To my friends, thank you for tolerating this weird poetry habit, and gilding my days with laughter.

To Kian and Adara Gallagher, who thinks it's cool their mother writes poetry, thank you for allowing me to be that mother, and for the first class ticket into your world of adventure and whimsy.

To Angus Gallagher for his unreserved support. My first and most faithful editor, who helped me find humour when agonizing over words and punctuation, supplied me with gallons of tea and who regularly emboldens all my dreams.

And finally, thank you to you, for holding this book and visiting with my thoughts for awhile. This is the absolute best bit of it all.

Poems in this collection which have previously appeared in the following publications;

"Spatial Awareness": *Not A Muse: A World Poetry Anthology* (2009)
"Soon To Be Named": *Not A Muse: A World Poetry Anthology* (2009)
"Tai O Village": *Outloud Too* (2013)

Nashua Gallagher is the founding director of Peel Street Poetry, a literary arts collective that have run spoken word sessions and other events in Hong Kong since 2005. Her work has previously been featured in *Not A Muse: A World Poetry Anthology* (2009), *Outloud Too* (2013), and *Asian Cha*. She has performed her poetry at several Hong Kong International Literary Festivals and TEDxWanchai's main stage event in 2016. By day, Nashua is a media professional.

She lives in Hong Kong with her husband, two children and growing menagerie of animals. This is her first book.

Lightning Source UK Ltd.
Milton Keynes UK
UKHW011227140720
366520UK00002B/647